SCHOOL RECESS

MARGO GATES

**GRL Consultants,
Diane Craig and Monica Marx,
Certified Literacy Specialists**

Lerner Publications ◆ Minneapolis

TABLE OF CONTENTS

School Recess 4

School Recess

Recess is a break
in the school day.
It is time for us
to play!

Some kids play soccer or basketball.

They make teams to play.

Other kids jump rope, play tag, or go on the swings.

**What do you do
at recess?**

Our teachers watch
us at recess.
They make sure we
play safe and fair.

We follow rules at recess.
We watch where we are
going when we run.

We look out
for others.
We tell a teacher
if someone
gets hurt.

Why do you think rules are important at recess?

We are kind at recess.

We play with everyone.
We take turns.

Our teacher blows a whistle at the end of recess.

We put away our balls and jump ropes.

We walk back to our classroom.
We are ready to learn more!

You Connect!

What do you like to do at recess?

What rules do you follow at recess?

How do you show kindness at recess?

Social and Emotional Snapshot

Student voice is crucial to building reader confidence. Ask the reader:

> What is your favorite part of this book?

> What is something you learned from this book?

> Did this book remind you of your own time at recess?

Opportunities for social and emotional learning are everywhere. How can you connect the topic of this book to the SEL competencies below?

Self-Awareness
Relationship Skills
Social Awareness

Photo Glossary

basketball

jump rope

swing

whistle

Learn More

Brozo, Patty. *The Buddy Bench*. Thomaston, ME: Tilbury House Publishers, 2019.

Gates, Margo. *Making Friends at School*. Minneapolis: Lerner Publishing, 2023.

Rustad, Martha E. H. *Michael Makes Friends at School*. Minneapolis: Millbrook Press, 2018.

Index

Photo Acknowledgments

The images in this book are used with the permission of: © Anant Jadhav/Shutterstock Images, p. 17; © FatCamera/iStockphoto, pp. 12–13; © GagliardiPhotography/Shutterstock Images, pp. 7, 20, 23 (basketball); © graphbottles/Shutterstock Images, pp. 18, 23 (whistle); © iofoto/iStockphoto, pp. 14–15; © Monkey Business Images/Shutterstock Images, pp. 6, 16; © omgimages/iStockphoto, pp. 10–11; © Ridofranz/iStockphoto, pp. 19, 23 (jump rope); © Robert Kneschke/Shutterstock Images, pp. 4–5; © Sergey Novikov/Shutterstock Images, pp. 8–9, 23 (swing).

Cover Photo: TinnaPong/Shutterstock Images.

Design Elements: © Mighty Media, Inc.

Lerner Publications Company
An imprint of Lerner Publishing Group, Inc.
241 First Avenue North
Minneapolis, MN 55401 USA

For reading levels and more information, look up this title at www.lernerbooks.com.

Main body text set in Mikado a Medium.
Typeface provided by Hannes von Doehren.

Library of Congress Cataloging-in-Publication Data

Names: Gates, Margo, author.
Title: School recess / Margo Gates.
Description: Minneapolis : Lerner Publications, [2023] | Series: Read about School (Read for a Better World) | Audience: Ages 5–8 years | Audience: Grades K–1 | Summary: "Recess is many kids' favorite part of the school day. Kid-friendly information on safety and expected behavior make this book perfect for young learners"– Provided by publisher.
Identifiers: LCCN 2021043410 (print) | LCCN 2021043411 (ebook) | ISBN 9781728459325 (Library Binding) | ISBN 9781728464251 (Paperback) | ISBN 9781728461861 (eBook)
Subjects: LCSH: School recess breaks—Juvenile literature.
Classification: LCC LB3033 .G38 2023 (print) | LCC LB3033 (ebook) | DDC 371.2/42–dc23/eng/20211027

LC record available at https://lccn.loc.gov/2021043410
LC ebook record available at https://lccn.loc.gov/2021043411

Manufactured in the United States of America
1 – CG – 7/15/22